Cockatoos

Set II

AF430451

Table of Contents

WRITTEN BY KASSI GILMOUR

"Cocky want a cracker?" is a saying that many cockatoos have chirped.

These smart birds can be trained to mimic speech, and are known for a few iconic quotes.

Hello cocky

Want a cracker?

3

Classify

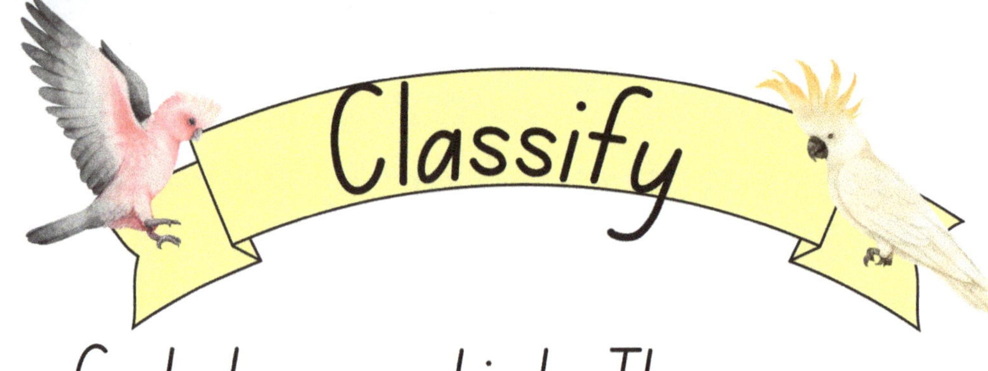

Cockatoos are birds. They are part of the parrot family. There are around twenty different types of cockatoos.

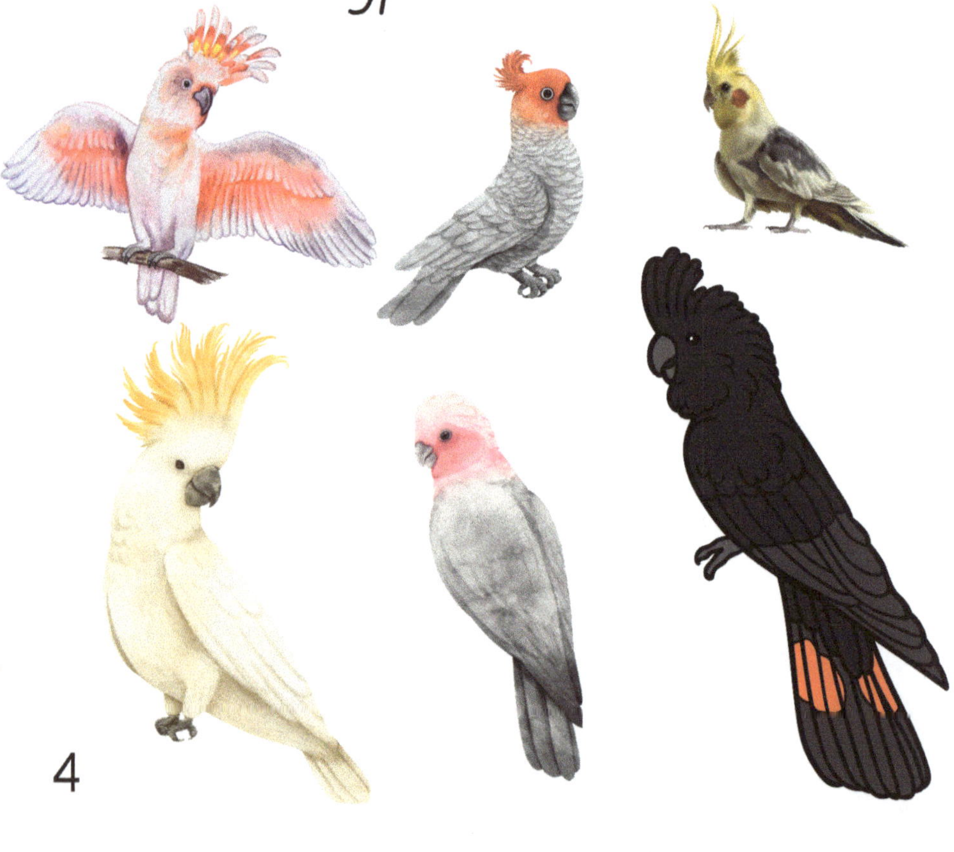

White cockatoos are the most popular and iconic type of cockatoo.

Black cockatoos are often bigger than other types.

There are a few types of cockatoos that are different shades of pink.

6

Cockatoos are crested parrots. Their crest opens out like a fan.

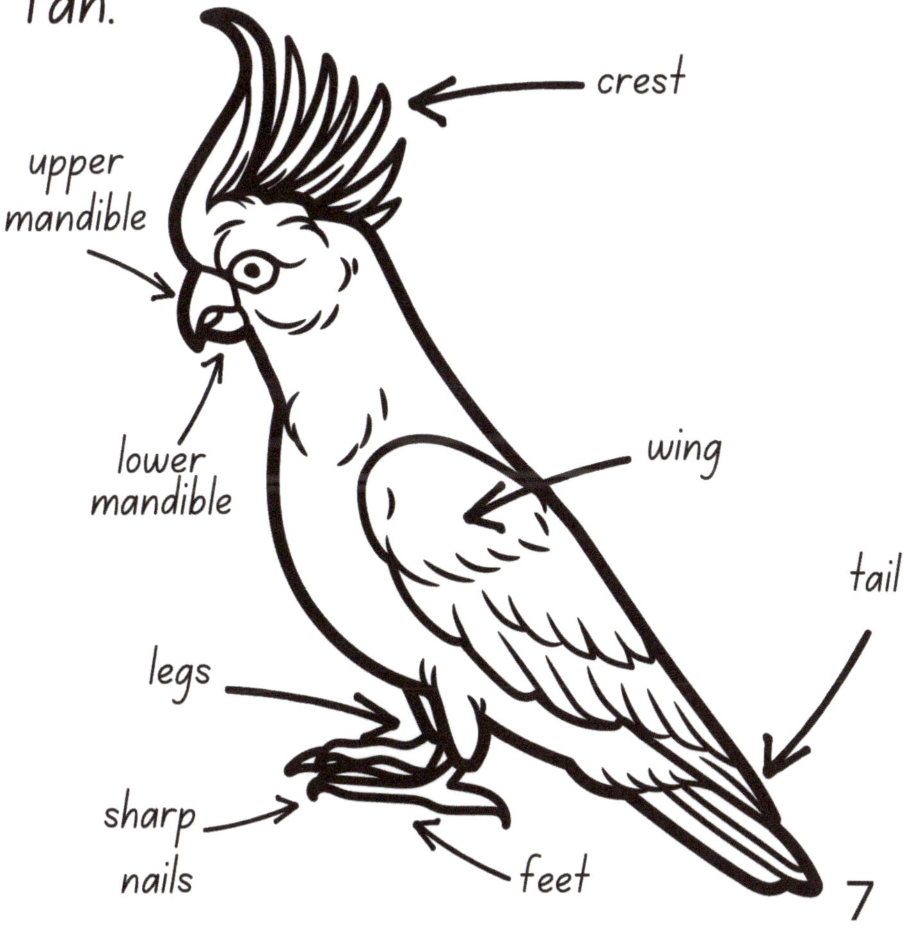

Many of them are white, with bits of yellow and red under their wings and in their tails. Other cockatoos are black and pink.

All cockatoos have dark curved beaks, called the upper and lower mandibles. They are strong and capable of cracking open hard nuts.

Their long crests sit on top of the bird's skull.

They have short legs and strong nails. The shape of their feet enables the cockatoo to pick up and manipulate food and objects.

Cockatoos are mid to big-sized birds.

Habitat

Cockatoos are only found on a small part of our planet.

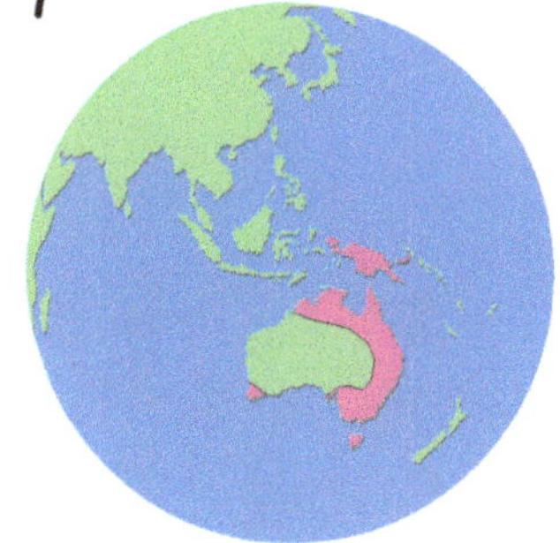

They can be seen in forests, farmlands, coastal mangroves, dry climates and highly populated suburbs.

Many cockatoos enjoy being with other birds and live together in massive gangs called flocks.

They roost and nest in hollow trunks at the tops of trees.

Because they are loving and showy birds, cockatoos make good pets. Pet cockatoos can live in homes.

Lots of room and toys are needed to keep these smart birds happy.

Cockatoos eat insects and plants. This includes grubs, grains, seeds, nuts, roots and leaf buds.

They can be a problem for farmers trying to grow grain crops.

Habits

Cockatoos are very noisy birds that let out loud screeches. This makes them easy to find. Approaching a flock of these wild birds is difficult. One flock member will stand on lookout duty and quickly alert the other birds if they suspect a risk.

Life

Male cockatoos will attract a female by strutting around with their crest raised. When he finds a mating partner, they work together to create a nest by chewing out an entry into a hollow tree.

One to three eggs are laid in the nest, and both birds take turns sitting on the eggs.

Little chicks are yellow and stay in the nest until it is time for them to exit.

Most cockatoo partners stay together for life. They can live as long as horses can.

Glossary

This page is not decodable and may be read to the child.

alert - to warn.
chicks - baby birds.
crest - a group of longer feathers found on a bird's head.
flock - a large group of birds.
hollow - empty space within a trunk.
mandible - part of a bird's bill.
mating partners - a pair that will breed.
nest - an area where eggs can be laid.
parrot - a curved bill bird that can mimic speech.
planet - the Earth.
screech - loud squawking.
strutting - a proud walk with the head raised and chest puffed out.

Index

Questions:

1. Describe a cockatoo.

2. Where do cockatoos live?

3. List some things cockatoos eat.

4. What would a pet cockatoo need?

5. What is an interesting fact that you have learned about cockatoos?

Vowels

The graphemes 'ur' and 'ir' represent the r-controlled vowel phoneme /er/, as in turn and girl.

The graphemes 'u_e' and 'ew' represent the long vowel phoneme /o͞o/, as in flute and drew.

These pictures help you remember the sound.

www.ingramcontent.com/pod-product-compliance
Lightning Source LLC
Chambersburg PA
CBHW041154150726
48006CB00015B/1977